Time To Be Unstoppable

Empowering Teenagers and Young Adults to Live the Life They Want

By Debbie van Dijk

Copyright © 2020 by Debbie van Dijk, Soul Decisions Coaching

All rights reserved.

The content contained within this book may not be reproduced, duplicated, or transmitted without direct written permission from the author or publisher. Under no circumstances will any blame or legal responsibility be held against the publisher or author, for any damages, reparation, or monetary loss due to the information contained within this book. Either directly or indirectly.

Legal Notice:

This book is copyright protected. This book is only for personal use. You cannot amend, distribute, sell, use, quote or paraphrase any part, or the content within this book, without consent of the author or publisher.

Disclaimer Notice:

Please note the information contained within this document is for educational and entertainment purposes only. All effort has been executed to present accurate, up to date, reliable, complete information. No warranties of any kind are declared or implied. Readers acknowledge that the author is not engaging in the rendering of legal, financial, medical, or professional advice. The content within this book has been derived from various sources. Please consult a licensed professional before attempting any techniques outlined in this book. By reading this document, the reader agrees that under no circumstances is the author responsible for any losses, direct or indirect, which are incurred as a result of the use of the information contained within this document, including, but not limited to, errors, omissions, or inaccuracies.

ISBN 978-0-473-52583-5

www.souldecisionscoaching.com

Acknowledgements

I would like to thank:

My amazing children, Emily and Matthew. This book is for you. You are the best. You teach me lessons every day, and I love you with all my heart. I want you both to live the best life possible. To know that you both have your own unique gifts to bring to this world. I'm so proud of you both.

My incredible husband, Dave, you have my heart and soul forever and always. Thank you for all the support you show, and the wise words when I've needed them.

My wonderful sister and business partner, Becky. You've helped me in so many ways. I love what we're creating together from different corners of the world. Thank you for guiding me through the technology and supporting me in completing this book. Many more to come xxx

Elo, my beautiful copywriter, and editor. You have the most brilliant ability with words. It's such a constant privilege to work with you. I trust you completely to keep me on the right track. Thank you for being a support through the writing of this book. I'm already looking forward to the next one. Check Elo out at www.helloelo.co.nz

Ant, my amazing graphic designer. I love your work and enthusiasm for what you do. You're incredible, always so efficient, so accommodating, and so much fun to be with. I love working with you. Check out the girls, Ant, and Noleen at www.SonsOfSerif.com

To the many role models I've had throughout my life. I'd like to thank all of you for having such a positive influence and guiding me in ways I would never have thought possible.

Table of contents

Acknowledgements 2
Table of contents 3
Becoming you 4
First, here's a little about me 7
So, where do we start? 9
How do you live your life now? 10
What do you value? 16
What do you believe? 19
The power of choice. 36
What are you thinking? 40
Meditation as a tool 42
You think you have time 44
CHOOSE to focus on the direction you want to go 45
Fear and excuses 48
Understanding the inner workings of the ego 59
Making decisions: the first step towards meaningful change 66
Things to be aware of when life feels tough 87
Conclusion 92
About Soul Decisions Coaching 94

Becoming you

Have you ever asked yourself, "Who am I"? Have you ever wondered what life's all about? Are you troubled by feelings of anxiety, loneliness, not being good enough, or not fitting in?

If so, this book was written for you. If I'd had a book like this when I was in my teens and early adulthood, my perception of life would have been so much clearer emotionally. I would have understood far sooner that, just like you, I've always been capable of discovering what I wanted for myself, and creating the life I wanted to lead.

To get to know and understand yourself, start by asking yourself some constructive questions. Questions like, "What do I want my life to be like? Why am I here? What's the point of my life? Why is this happening to me? Why can't I control certain things?" ...and the many more questions I'm sure you've been wanting to ask. These inner conflicts can drive us crazy sometimes. The more we focus on them, the more they grow and leave an imprint in our bodies. For some people, that imprint can last a lifetime. For others, the answers may never be found.

This book's goal is to get you thinking about your life and what you want for yourself both now and in the future. Most importantly, it will help you to live in the HERE and NOW. To form great habits and make sure your future is filled with courage and trust in yourself. To know for sure that whatever internal or external obstacles come your way, you can handle them. To be able to discover your solutions, instead of hiding away or being down on yourself.

If you've picked up this book, there's something in you that knows you're capable of more. You want more out of your life, and you deserve to live the best life possible. You've begun your journey into discovering, or even creating, who you want to be. Good on you. I'm proud of you, and I feel privileged to help you take that little spark inside of you that says, "there's more," and turn it into a roaring blazing fire. The fire that says, "I'm unstoppable. I'm here to live my best life possible. Move aside, I'm coming through regardless, and I'm willing to do what it takes to be who I want to be. I'm living my life full-out, with passion and purpose, and it feels AMAZING!!"

The questions in this book are there to inspire you to act. Have a notebook and pen ready. You might just want to write down some discoveries as you explore.

Enjoy the journey.

With love,

Deb

Make decisions NOW that your future self will be so grateful for.

First, here's a little about me

I thought I would start by sharing a piece of my history in case there's something in it you can relate to.

My childhood was filled with neglect, fear, and a lack of love, comfort, or security. My sisters and I didn't know if there would be food on the table, or who would provide for us. Our clothes were tatty and worn. My parents didn't keep up payments, so our home was taken away from us. Mum had a nervous breakdown. She wouldn't hear us speak, couldn't give us eye contact, and, most of the time, didn't seem to know we existed. She was in her own world, talking to imaginary strangers that appeared very real for her. Dad... well, one day, he was there, and the next, he was gone. No explanation, no discussion. Just gone.

I remember many years of searching for love and acceptance from somebody. As a teenager, I felt lost to the point of being depressed. I felt completely alone and lived in a daily state of fear and rejection. I was lost in anxiety, and I had no idea how to get out of it, or even what it was all about. I can't think of one happy childhood memory that could even begin to explain the strong, happy, fulfilled, fun, committed, loyal, trustworthy woman I am today. So, where did she come from?

I believe she came from an innate sense that there was more to life. I somehow knew that I was meant to be a somebody. That I had the right to live the best life possible, and that I had to find out what that was for myself. That I had to push through the neglect, abuse, and fear of not being accepted for who I was. Through the lack of love, self-belief, value for my existence, or anyone to turn to.

Tony Robbins, a renowned author, and life coach, once said, "What if Life happens FOR you, not TO you." I spent so many wasted years blaming my childhood for a lack of things in my life. But today, I see that my childhood happened for me, not to me. Looking back, I can honestly say I learned some incredible lessons. I've learned to appreciate all of it because it made me who I am today.

I know that if you've picked up this book, you're curious about how you can become more. That you're looking to be bigger and better, and successful now and in your future. Before you can do that, you need to know what success means to you. What does success look like in your life? I used to think it was about wealth because I came from a poverty-stricken background where money always seemed unattainable. If that's what you're thinking too, then let me tell you now; it's not about money.

It's about the person you become on your journey to discovering you. It's about you discovering your own inner strength, confidence, joy, peace, happiness, fulfilment, and living life on your terms.

If money is important to you, then that will flow.

So, where do we start?

We start with your burning desire for something different, something more out of life. Do you have a burning desire inside yourself? A knowing that you can do and be so much more? Do you have the sense that you'll only go so far before retreating? Are you hiding yourself from full view? Hiding from fully experiencing life, because you might be seen? Do you feel like you should fit in, or are you secretly comparing yourself to others? Have you got so many amazing ideas that just keep getting squashed, and somehow you just can't bring them into reality?

Thoughts and feelings like these can stop you from living the life you want. They can stop you from being your true self, or discovering who that true self is – because you're so busy trying to be someone else.

These feelings can seem quite normal to you. They're the way things are and always have been. So you just learn to live with them. But over time, they eat away at your self-worth and confidence and prevent you from reaching out. You feel like you're different from everyone else. You can't ask for help because you see it as a sign of weakness. You think you're different, or you're not as good as some of your friends. You feel like you never say the right thing, or you're scared people will make fun of you, so you don't speak up at all.

It takes courage to let yourself step outside the box

Not conforming to who or what other people think you should be also takes courage, especially when your life is filled with influential relationships. To stand strong in your sense of who you are and what you want out of your life can and will take courage.

Know for a fact that you have everything you need to succeed in life, right now, inside yourself. You always have, and you always will have. It's how you access that self-belief that counts, and then what you do with it.

This book will help show you the way. It's not complicated; the tools ahead are simple to use and quick to implement. What makes the difference is how committed you are to discovering your answers, being true to yourself, and following through. Making decisions now and keeping up your focus will help you create the outcome you want; a better life. Staying committed is the key — not just when things are flowing nicely, but when obstacles undoubtedly come.

How do you live your life now?

I was introduced to the "above/ below the line" concept a few years ago, and it was a turning point of realization in my life.

The concept is based on the idea that we can all think about and respond to events in our lives with either open positivity (above the line) or closed negativity (below the line).

So... how do you choose to live your life?

Above The Line – Ownership, Responsibility, Accountability

Having ownership, taking responsibility, and being accountable for our behaviour means we have more control over our lives. We tend to be happier and much more successful when we live our lives with above the line behaviours.

Below The Line – Blame, Denial, Excuses, Justifications

Blaming others, being in denial, making excuses, and justifying our actions leads to unhappiness, anger, resentment, ill feelings, and even depression. You think you have little or no control over your life.

An exercise: above the line/below the line thinking

Take a moment to stop and ask yourself, am I living my life above the line or below the line?

If you're living below the line, ask yourself why. What would it take to move yourself above the line? Use this space for your thoughts.

_____

_____

_____

_____

_____

If you want a different reality for your life, you must think differently and act differently

A successful life: what to let go of and what to embrace

Let go of:

- Gossip
- Family arguments
- The need to be the centre of attention
- The need to conform to the expectations of others
- The need to prove you're right
- The need to please everyone
- The need to prove yourself

Fully embrace:

- Your values
- Your vision
- Your dreams
- Your life
- Your peace

Learning to love obstacles

The obstacles that come to you are there for you to push through, so you can discover your inner strength and wisdom. Obstacles exist to show you that you already have it within you to push through and discover a new level of confidence on the other side.

I don't believe that people should suffer in life. But I do believe that out of suffering, greatness can evolve, and your true self can be revealed. You can learn what you're capable of if you're willing, determined, focused, and committed to living your best life possible – no matter what your background.

Even if you had the best childhood possible – and I truly hope you did – I can still guarantee that there's room to grow and learn.

"Just Keep Going. Your life is worth it."

— Soul Decisions Coaching

What do you value?

Our values are like our emotional compass. When we're not living by our values, life certainly feels rocky. Relationships struggle. We begin to question what we're doing and why things aren't going the way we want them to. This can go on for years before finally, we've had enough, and we make a change.

We all have our own set of values, either conscious or unconscious

When we live by our personal values, life flows. That's why, if you're living your life by the standards of others, something probably doesn't feel right to you. You may find yourself doing what people expect of you or comparing yourself to others.

When we share the same values, our relationships flourish. Accepting others' values as different to our own, while also maintaining our own values, keeps us living the standard of life we want to live. Compatibility happens when we're a value match, or when we learn to accept differences. Not when we lower our standards to suit other people or expect others to lower theirs.

The trouble is, most people have no idea what their values are – which means they don't even realize they're not living by them. This can show up when you feel a wrong decision has been made, but you still let it happen. It can show up in relationships when you feel uneasy with someone but still let them into your life. When you let yourself be treated a certain way, or you go along with something you know isn't right for you.

Does any of that ring a bell for you? Then it might be time for you to uncover your values.

An exercise: discovering your values.

Take a look at the values below. Write down any that resonate for you, and explore why.

Compassion, Trust, Wellness, Respect, Family, Kindness, Empathy, Love, Loyalty, Connection, Gratitude, Teamwork, Authenticity, Forgiveness, Integrity, Wisdom, Security, Persistence, Humour, Spirituality, Strength, Open-mindedness, Creativity, Generosity, Knowledge, Leadership, Confidence, Community, Tenacity, Bravery, Beauty, Inclusion, Resilience, Ethics, Independence, Adventure, Self-Growth, Humility, Love of Learning, Collaboration, Courage, Assertiveness, Resourcefulness, Balance, Commitment, Passion, Curiosity, Vitality, Fun, Change, Fairness, Perspective, Responsibility, Wealth, Environment, Culture.

"Are you living your life by your standards or by the standards of others?"

- Soul Decisions Coaching

What do you believe?

Our thoughts are beliefs, and beliefs are shaped by our life experience. By what people tell us about ourselves, and what *we* tell ourselves. Some of those beliefs may be positive; others limit us and hold us back from reaching our potential.

Our limiting beliefs sit in our subconscious. That means we're not even aware of them until we're triggered by something that we believe to be true, but others may not. We might try to convince someone to our way of thinking, or try to persuade someone to believe what we believe. This may not turn out as we'd hope, because their beliefs are different from ours.

You might have experienced this during a disagreement with a parent or a friend. In these situations, how accepting are you of a difference of opinion? How distressing is it when you can only see your point of view and only the certainty of your beliefs? If you could think differently and consider the beliefs of the other person, would it ease some of that distress?

I've said this already – but it's so important, I'll say it again here:

If you want a different reality for your life, you must think differently and act differently.

Limiting beliefs subconsciously rule our everyday lives

Many people go about their day, limiting themselves through subconscious fears. But when we listen to our bodies, we realize those fears reveal themselves on a physical level. This brings the need to act to our attention, so we can resolve whatever it is that pains us.

Next time your inner voice speaks to you, take a moment to reflect. What are you thinking? What's going on in your head? What's going on in your body? Are those voices giving you fuel for your fire? Or are they like a bucket of water being thrown over the fire, to extinguish any spark, surge of energy, or a good idea or thought? Is your first reaction to see the barrier, or is it to see the possible solution?

Our minds and bodies are so inextricably linked. Our thoughts create a chemical reaction in our bodies and, over time, leave a blueprint. We become addicted to certain beliefs that we're <u>convinced</u> are right, even if they don't do us any favours.

Let's look at some examples

Think back to a time in your life when you felt excited about something. Your mind was telling you how brilliant it was, and your body was giving you physical responses, wasn't it? You felt so energised and full of life, your heart was racing, you were filled with positivity, you smiled and laughed easily. You told yourself this was so right for you, and you instinctively knew it to be true. You felt untouchable, unstoppable.

Then imagine a moment when you felt sad or frustrated. Your mind was telling you stories to reinforce those feelings, and you became stuck there. It became a loop of negative emotional energy, continuously reinforced from within. A loop of thought and feeling, repeated until it became your blueprint and your way of being.

You may know people like this. They don't smile very often. They take everything so seriously, have forgotten how to laugh and have fun, and often answer with a negative comment or see the problem and never the solution. They have difficulty communicating in relationships. They feel lost and empty, filled with uncertainty. This could even resonate with you as you read it. This could even be you.

It doesn't have to be that way

No worries. No dramas. This can change – IF you want it to. Do you want it to? I think you must; otherwise, you probably wouldn't be reading this book! I applaud you for being so amazing and looking for something else. Something different, something new, and maybe even something challenging.

I'll repeat; no worries, no dramas. These thoughts are all created IN YOUR HEAD. They're stories you're telling yourself. You're standing in your own way. So let's change the stories, and create a quiet confidence within you. Your life is amazing, your body is amazing, and you have a purpose to fulfil in this lifetime. An impact to have on this world. What legacy will you leave?

An exercise: creating new beliefs

Now, there's something I'd like you to do. When you discover something new that you like about yourself, I want you to hold onto it for dear life – until it becomes so natural to you that you don't need to hold on so hard anymore.

Better yet, write it down and keep it as a visual reminder.

Please, please do this. No matter how much you want to fall back into old habits, guard those new habits and beliefs with your life. Trust me; you'll never regret it.

What I love about myself:

An exercise: identifying your beliefs

Our belief system comes from the experiences we have and what we're told. So let's take a look at what your current beliefs are, and question how well they serve you in the life you want to lead.

Give yourself the time and space to do this exercise without interruptions. Answer each sentence quickly, and do your best not to overthink it.

Please answer the following:

I always

_____

_____

_____

_____

I never

_____

_____

_____

I am

They are

We are

I can't

I must

My life is

Spend a little time with these beliefs. Be curious and explore how they line up with who you want to be.

Which would you change? What would you change them to?
_____
_____
_____
_____

Share these beliefs with someone you trust. Talk them through, and turn any negative beliefs into positive ones. Beliefs that will help you gain confidence. No more false stories that hold you back or make you feel sad and lonely. You have a choice here, so take it.

Imagine how amazing you'll feel when you adopt beliefs that empower you!!!

Here are a few more beliefs to explore.

Please answer the following:

If I try hard then
_____
_____
_____

Life is about

Love is about

If I'm responsible, then

There are times when life

People are

My family always

It takes …. to be successful

…is outside my control

There is no such thing as

My friends are

_____

_____

_____

_____

My Mum is / My Dad is

_____

_____

_____

_____

I am stressed when

_____

_____

_____

_____

I am happy when
_____
_____
_____
_____

I am sad when
_____
_____
_____
_____

I could
_____
_____
_____
_____

I am scared when

I Love

I get angry when

The important things in my life are

...loves me

I want

Success is

_____

_____

_____

_____

I fear

_____

_____

_____

_____

Look at what you've written. Your answers are your beliefs.

Have you written positive words or negative? If they're negative in nature, try replacing them with something positive. Rewrite them with the life you want to lead in mind.

"The definition of insanity is doing the same thing over and over again and expecting a different result."

Albert Einstein

The power of choice.

Think about all the great choices you've made in your life. Those that made you feel happy and excited.

Next, think about the present and future choices you'll make to help create the life you want.

Now think about all those small daily choices you make that <u>don't</u> serve you. Those that make you feel uncomfortable. These can be simple, everyday choices that have just become a habit for you. Choices like talking about someone behind their back, comparing yourself to someone else, or spending hours on screens instead of time with others. How can you make a different choice, to help create the life you want to live?

An exercise: changing your choices.

Write down your choices so you have a visual representation, and focus on them one by one. It really doesn't matter how small the choice is; change your choices, and your life will change too.

_____

_____

_____

_____

_____

> "Change isn't by chance; it's by CHOICE."
>
> — Sharon Pearson

It's your choice.

I choose how I feel.

I choose what I do.

I choose what I want.

I choose what I will tolerate.

I choose what I don't want.

I choose my actions.

I choose who I spend time with.

I choose what I eat.

I choose what I like.

I choose where I go.

Your life, your choice. Choose wisely!

"Choose JOY! Don't wait for things to get easier, simpler, better. Life will always be complicated. Learn to be happy right NOW. Otherwise, you will run out of time. We can't often choose our circumstances, but we can better control our reactions and emotions. Choose JOY."

Unknown

What are you thinking?

Are you aware of your thoughts? Are they kind to you? Would you speak to your friends, family, girlfriend, or boyfriend the way your thoughts speak to you?

Is there a thought that keeps repeating itself to you, over and over again, so that now you're convinced it's your truth?

Could this thought have created a limiting belief that now holds you back?

> *"Your thoughts and your feelings create your life. It will always be that way. Guaranteed!"*
>
> — Lisa Nichols

An exercise: observing your thoughts

The following exercise is my interpretation of an activity from Arjuna Ishaya's book '200%: An Instruction Manual for Living Fully.'

Get comfortable, and let's get started.

For just a few moments, stop and observe your thoughts.

Watch them. Notice them. Gently let them come, then let them go.

Just because you have thoughts, it doesn't mean they're true.

They can just be an idea, a label, an interpretation, an option, or an opinion.

A thought can just be passing energy.

There's no need to link emotion to it.

Observe and let go. Observe and let go.

You are <u>not</u> your thoughts.

They don't need to define or limit you in any way.

You have a **choice**…………**Always.**

Meditation as a tool

I know so many teenagers and young adults who suffer from anxiety and stress and find it hard to cope with life. For these people, I always recommend meditation.

Meditation is an amazing tool at your disposal at any time of the day or night. There are lots of meditation styles and options to choose from. One I highly recommend is Ascension, as taught by Ishayas of The Bright Path. It's so simple, easy to use, and truly life-transforming. In fact, the exercise on the previous page – 'observing your thoughts' – comes from a Bright Path teacher.

Thinking about your life in 'above the line' terms, your decision to meditate is you taking responsibility for your own inner peace and stillness. When you can go to this place easily, you'll gain so much more clarity, contentment, confidence, and freedom. You'll feel so much more stable and grounded, be less reactive to situations, more creative, and have more love, joy, and happiness. You won't feel the need to compare yourself to (or gossip about) other people anymore. The people around you will feel your calmness. You'll learn how to create the future you want, and still stay in the present moment. The beautiful time that we call 'now.' Meditation is such an effective way to let go of the worries that crowd your thoughts and disturb your emotions.

Here are a few of my top meditation recommendations:

Watch:
Start by taking a look at the film 'A Mindful Choice.'
Visit The Choice Film to learn more.

Read:
'Boundless' by Greg Hopkinson.
'200%: An Instruction Manual For Healthy Living' by Arjuna Ishaya.
'The Power of Now' by Eckhart Tolle.

If you're interested in attending a workshop to learn the Ascension technique, visit www.thebrightpath.com. Here you'll find lots of information and a calendar of events and training in your area.

You think you have time

We have an abundance of time. It's how we spend that time that matters. Have you noticed that some people just seem to get so much done, and look so calm and collected – but others are massively stressed out, busy not achieving much at all? Have you ever wondered why? How?

I feel that managing your time is a fundamental lesson to learn in life. It's so important to know how to use your time wisely, so you can achieve everything you want to accomplish without the added stress.

Have you ever thought about the fact that time is one thing we all have in common? We all have the same amount of it. Time brings out so much emotion in us. It creates pressure; the idea of things we should have done in the past, should be doing right now, or must do in the future.

When we link an emotion to time, life seems so much more challenging. How often have you said, "I haven't got enough time to do that"? What emotion are you feeling in that moment? Are you down on yourself? Does it feel heavy? Does it feel like a burden? Does it feel like you're just not good enough? Does it feel stressful and overwhelming? Does it sometimes even make you tear up? If this is what you focus on, you'll only end up feeling more stressed and overwhelmed. You'll waste even more time feeling bad about yourself. And as if you weren't feeling emotionally bad enough already, your body will even start releasing lots of nasty chemical gremlins to make you feel physically bad, too!

But don't worry. There's a way out of this hamster wheel, and it sounds simple – because it is.

CHOOSE to focus on the direction you want to go

We all have things in life that we don't want to do but have to. Flip your perspective by CHOOSING to do it. Just do it. Stop overthinking and decide to do it, now. If you practice this, you'll realize that getting on and doing it takes a fraction of the energy you spend worrying about putting it off.

Step one: What do you want your result to be? What's the outcome you want from the task? I want you to visualize the task finished, and feel the emotion you'll feel when it's done. Use your imagination.

Step two: Why do you want to get this task done? What's your compelling 'why'? This will be the driving force that propels you to keep going, so it has to be strong. Do the task with your outcome and reason for doing it top of mind. See it finished, and feel the feelings that will go along with getting it done.

Step three: Create an action plan with simple steps. Tiny little steps are better than no steps at all. Then focus, focus, focus through every obstacle in the way. Don't take your focus off the task, or you won't finish it. Remember; commitment, persistence, and focus.

Step one: What do you want your result to be? What's the outcome you want from the task?

Step two: Why do you want to get this task done? What's your compelling 'why'?

Step three: Create an action plan with simple steps.

"The walls of your comfort zone are lovingly decorated with your lifelong collection of favourite excuses."

– Jen Sincero

Fear and excuses

If you knew you could handle whatever life threw at you, what would you try to achieve?

Fear holds us back when we think about our challenges and let the fear grow. The more we think about it, the bigger it gets. We're giving it focus and attention – and, therefore, fuel. We get what we focus on! You know this to be true.

Think about something you've wanted. How much focus and attention did you give that thing before it finally became yours? When you wanted to finish a task, and you just focused on that one task, did you get it done? Describe it here:

Are you waiting to be confident before you act?

Excuses stop us from stretching ourselves in life, and it's so easy to fall into the fear trap. "I can't do that because I haven't got the skill, the time… I'm too busy…if only you knew what I was going through… I'm so tired…" …on and on the list goes. Then there's the hidden fear of, "I'm not good enough, they're judging me, you don't love me." The more excuses you make, the more you lose confidence. Fear is part of life. Everyone experiences it on some level. Everyone. It's inevitable.

We experience courage and confidence when we act despite our fear.

The more we do the challenging thing, the less we see it as a challenge. The more we face challenges, the more we grow. We get to the next level of living, where we can let ourselves face bigger and better challenges.

Imagine what it would feel like if you welcomed that fear because you knew it was going to lead you to bigger and better things in life.

When we make excuses, we honestly believe what we're telling ourselves. We can truly convince ourselves these excuses are valid. But the truth is, we've created them to prevent us from facing fear. We use them to justify why we should or shouldn't do something. What are you telling yourself in those moments?

What solution-focused words can you use instead?

_____

_____

_____

Give yourself the gift of a different choice.

When you look at your excuses with an open mind, you can give yourself a different perspective. This new perspective can then create a different outcome and change the whole direction of your life. You'll find confidence and courage when you face the fear and walk through it to the other side of the experience. Confidence and courage won't come until you do.

Give yourself a different reason to face your fear. It could be that you know you'll feel empowered; you'll become unstoppable; you'll create so many opportunities for yourself.

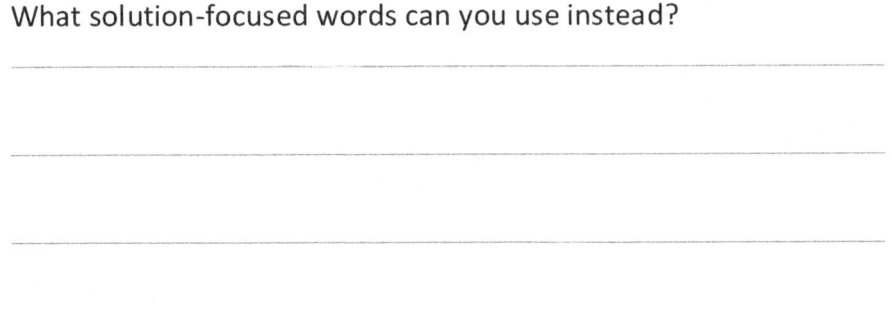

An exercise: be fearless.

When you do this exercise, it helps to tune into your body. Take note of how you feel when you're about to stop yourself doing something by making an excuse.

The feeling tends to be uncomfortable. It could be a feeling in your stomach, your gut, a tightness in your shoulders, or a change in your breathing.

"Be afraid and jump anyway into life. The life you want to live."

- Lisa Nichols

First, try this little warm-up – and have some fun with it.

Let's just say you could have anything you wanted. Imagine how your life would be if you had no fear. No little voices are telling you what to do. No past limiting beliefs robbing you of your amazing future.

Instead, you make decisions quickly and easily. You feel fearless, strong, unstoppable, determined, committed.

Now, here we go!

"I am fearless, strong, unstoppable."

Look at the above sentence, and don't just read it. Get into the FEELING of it. Feel it and imagine it. Really feel it, and believe the truth and power of it, until it feels real. Put on some music that pumps you up, to help get you into a state of high energy and positivity. (Some of the best athletes in the world do this, so don't feel silly!).

Are you doing it? Good!

If not, put this book down for a few minutes. Close your eyes, until you feel it so strongly that you want to scream 'YESSSSSSSSSS' and punch the air. You've got this. Is somebody watching? Great, an audience!

Do it again. This time, get your audience to join in.

Life is for living, and you are fearless

As you read this, imagine courageous feelings coursing through your body. Stand tall. Put your shoulders back. Hold your head high and breathe deeply and purposefully. It's especially important to put your body in an assertive and powerful posture, not closed-up or slumped with round shoulders. Do whatever you have to do to convince yourself of your power.

Allow yourself the experience of fearless freedom.

What a beautiful, life-transforming gift you can give yourself by doing this. Create a story in your mind, and a physical feeling in your body that fills you up, and sends positivity coursing through you.

Feel a sense of total belief in yourself, your creativity, your strength, and your life. Your beautiful and exciting life - full of joy, fun, passion, connection, health, and wealth. And YOU created all of it.

An exercise: creating the life you want through action

Now take this new feeling, and choose something you want to do that you've been putting off. Write the thing down. Then act on it.

Next, make a list of all the things you want to do – and really let go with this one. Be as adventurous as you can be. Remember, you're fearless, strong, unstoppable, determined, and committed to your future. Your life is for living.

Go wild with your wishes and desires for the best life ever. This is your only life. Search your soul. Live the life you are meant to live.

Make your unstoppable, courageous list now.

Leaning into fearful feelings

Is there a way you could learn to love fear? What would it give you if you could feel the fear and do whatever you wanted anyway?

The more you step into those things that scare you, the more you'll grow. Think of the proof you've already seen of this in your life. Remember a time when you did something even though it scared you. It's important to gain a deeper awareness and appreciation of that feeling, and acknowledge that it could lead to an experience that will change your life. That it has in the past and will do again in the future.

The more you can do this for yourself, the more you will grow trust in yourself, and the more adventurous and amazing your life will be.

The physicality and language of fear

When you experience fear, are you aware of the physical sensations in your body? Does your stomach churn, heart race, blood pump, and breathing deepen?

Now, here's a handy little trick. What if you could use language to turn that fear into something else? Like excitement, anticipation, or courage?

Change the name, and the feelings associated with it will change along with it.

Words of wisdom from your soul.

"Today and every day, let what you are doing be enough. Allow judgments you have about what you 'should' or 'could' be doing to fall away. Allow yourself to simply be in this moment. Breathe gently.

Let go of the voice that tells you to do more, and be more, and rest in stillness.
All is well.
Trust that in this and every moment...
You are enough."

- Soul Decisions Coaching

Understanding the inner workings of the ego

The ego is our beliefs about who and what we are. It's a constructed identity of our own making, and it plays a significant role in shaping our personality and motivations.

It can also be a slippery little character. The ego operates from a place of fear, which is why it likes to keep us safe. It loves sameness, which is why it protects us from diving into new challenges.

The ego: above and below the line

Remember reading about 'above the line/below the line' earlier in this book? Well, each need of the ego can be met either above the line or below the line. Understanding both sides will help you understand certain behaviours you have that don't help you in life, versus those behaviours that do.

Here's a quick reminder of what above the line and below the line behaviours look like:

Resourceful (above the line):
Ownership | Accountability | Responsibility

Unresourceful (below the line):
Denial | Blame | Excuses | Justifications

The question is, where do you sit with each – and do you want that to change? If you do, will it bring more peace and joy into your life? Being able to let go of each of these needs, and live above the line consistently, will do just that. Try it out.

The six fundamental needs of the ego

The ego operates on six interlinked needs, based on fear and survival instincts that have been part of human nature for thousands of years.

1) The need to know

2) The need to judge

3) The need to justify

4) The need to be right

5) The need to look good

6) The need to get even

When you're aware of the six needs, you can become more aware of when you're acting from your head and not from your heart. This awareness leads to a whole different quality of conversation and interaction with others, and with yourself.

The ego's needs explained

1. The need to know

This is when you need absolute certainty, and want to have all the information before you act. This is the ego keeping you safe but also keeping you from moving forward in life. Figure out how to move away from this need. Say yes, and embrace uncertainty.

2. The need to judge

Judging yourself, others, and past and present situations will stop you from growing into the person you're meant to be. Notice how the ego is keeping you static. Notice how it stops you from being open to possibilities. Notice the pain you feel, or the discomfort in your body when you're judging someone, something, or yourself. Notice what you're doing and make a different choice. Let go of the judgment – and let whatever it is just be.

3. The need to justify

This is the need to justify both to others and yourself. We can talk ourselves into and out of situations, and convince ourselves that we're in the right. The thing is, there's usually a sinking feeling that goes with it. A physical knowing that something isn't quite right. Resourceful justification would be to listen to the body's innate understanding and act accordingly.

4. The need to be right

When you need to be right about everything, to prove and defend your opinions, you often override other people. You're right; they're not. Your opinion matters, theirs doesn't. For some people, this can be a fierce need. It's an unattractive energy, and often builds tension in relationships. It favours the need for control over understanding others and reading the room. Try accepting other people's opinions gracefully, instead. Approach life with curiosity. Show compassion to yourself, your family, your friends, even strangers – and let it go.

5. The need to look good

Below the line, this need shows up as a person driven by significance. Someone who puts others down to make themselves look good, and feels the need to put themselves in a position of power. Above the line, this helps us look after ourselves. It becomes a need to take pride in how we present ourselves to the world and influences others to look after themselves, too.

6. The need to get even

This need is about payback. Unresourcefully, this is about score-keeping, and getting even when we feel we've been wronged. Resourcefully, it can be getting even with yourself – for example, beating your highest score in a test, or striving to do something better than you did it before.

Letting go of judgement

How can we tell if we're judging something or someone?

Well, usually, there's an uncomfortable feeling that goes along with judgement. You can feel it in your body physically. There's an experience of struggle within. You become paralyzed by what you think something should be, instead of appreciating or accepting what is.

For some people, this can last a long time. It can ruin a lot of great relationships and even tear families apart.

An exercise: replacing judgement with curiosity

If you're hurting from something that's happened, try to change your awareness about it. Look at it with curiosity.

Ask yourself – has this happened to teach me something? And if so, what could that be? How could this help me grow?

Think of a time this has happened to you recently, and jot some thoughts down. As you're doing this exercise, remember to be gentle with yourself, and show yourself compassion.

Turning from the head to the heart

The ego doesn't run from the heart; it runs from the head. A heart-led life takes more courage and bravery. More stepping out of our comfort zone, more willingness to take on new challenges, more facing things we haven't come across before.

A heart-led life means deep, meaningful, beautiful, and reciprocal relationships – and a better understanding of who we are and what we stand for. If you live life resourcefully through your ego, you'll truly become an inspiration to yourself and others. You'll gain a deeper trust in yourself and become more committed to living your best life possible.

> *"I have no special talent. I am only passionately curious."*
>
> \- Albert Einstein

"Create and choose the mindset you want to live by. A mindset that is rich and abundant in health, wealth, and happiness."

- Soul Decisions Coaching

Making decisions: the first step towards meaningful change

You already know you're capable of making great decisions. After all, you decided to read this book! Staying on that track, and growing into your full potential, takes an upgrade in both your thinking and your actions.

It's about knowing what you want (or what you want to change), then deciding to rise up, lift your standards, and become the person you need to be to create the reality you want.

It takes courage to change your world

We humans often want all our 'ducks in a row' before deciding to create change. But in reality, there'll be times when you need to make the decision first, and trust that the rest will fall into place. That's why becoming a new you takes a rise in your awareness, curiosity, determination, courage, commitment, and bravery – to name but a few.

As you start to make changes, you'll get a sneak peek into who you're capable of being. You'll notice a shift in energy. This can feel uncomfortable and intense at first – but those feelings will ease as your confidence grows.

Recognize, listen, and act

We all experience epiphanies in life. Lightbulb moments. Ideas that spring up when we least expect it. Change and moments like these go hand in hand. So when they happen, take action; don't just sit on it. Write it down so that you don't lose it.

Realize the choices you have, and act. Remember that your life can change, and you're totally capable of rising to the challenge. Pay attention or stay stuck. Create awareness for yourself.

The answer is inside of you, always.

"You will never change your life until you change something you do daily."

- John Maxwell

Here are a few steps to help create a new you

1. Ask yourself, "what can I do differently today?"
2. Make decisions quickly and follow through even when it seems hard.
3. Invest in yourself.
4. Be the person leading the way.
5. Have an "I can do it" attitude.
6. Believe it's possible. Tell yourself it's possible. Repeat, repeat, repeat.
7. Ask yourself - what could you say YES to, before you've figured out how you're going to do it?
8. Keep believing in yourself.
9. Never give up on yourself.
10. Surround yourself with the right people – the people who support you and who you can support right back.
11. Dream big.
12. Choose not to listen to the naysayers.
13. Find yourself a few people who you look up to and model them.

"Extraordinary people are ordinary people making extraordinary decisions."

– Sharon Pearson

Make decisions with confidence and courage

When we find the courage to make decisions, we build more confidence. And the more confidence we build, the more courageous decisions we're ready to make in the future.

Don't wait for confidence to come. Make brave decisions and commit to following them through, and confidence will be waiting for you on the other side.

What courageous decisions have you made in your life?

How did you feel when you were making them?

After you made them, how did you feel?

_____

_____

_____

What did those decisions give you?

_____

_____

_____

The next step in your life is only one decision away. What will you decide to do next?

The biggest change can come from the smallest daily steps

Are you taking daily actions to get your life moving in the right direction? Or are you waiting for everything to be perfect before you act?

Think of something in your life that you've been struggling to move forward, and ask yourself why. Be as honest with yourself as you can.

Think about your thoughts, feelings, and body sensations when exploring your answer. Sit with them for a little while, and be curious about how they impact your life.

Now think about the end result. How do you want this situation to turn out?

_____

_____

_____

_____

What small step(s) could you take to get that result? List them all.

_____

_____

_____

_____

What would it cost you to take the very first step?

_____

_____

_____

Now, what would it cost you to take no steps at all?

_____

_____

_____

There's more risk in staying still than in creating change

Some people live, work, or play in environments that are toxic to their health. Yet, for a whole range of reasons, they stay in those environments — leading to sickness, lack of motivation, and the stripping away of confidence, self-esteem, and self-belief. It's so detrimental to life.

Sometimes it takes all the strength you can muster to get yourself out of a situation. To let go of a friend who brings you down, or say goodbye to a sport or hobby that doesn't bring you joy anymore. But so often, the pain of staying is even worse than the pain of freeing yourself.

It's only with action that you can create change

I asked a teenager recently how much she wanted to see a change in her life. Her reply was 100% - but she wasn't taking any action to create the change she wanted so badly.

She needed the courage to take the first step.

Explore what's holding you back with honesty and courage, and you'll realize you already have the answers inside yourself.

And then you can take those steps towards change.

> "No matter how small you start, start something that matters."
>
> \- Brandon Matters

I love this quote. It's so simple but so powerful. If you look at most successful people in the world – people like Oprah, Albert Einstein, JK Rowling, and Tony Robbins – you'll find they started with nothing. They had many disadvantages in life that could have rendered them stuck. But they all chose to take something small and turn it into something huge. Something life-changing for themselves and others.

With a whole force of determination, failing, making mistakes, and picking themselves back up, they saw amazing results. What they wanted out of life mattered. What they do matters. They created enormous success and a fantastic legacy to leave behind, as well as having a colossal impact on the world.

What could you do to create a life that truly feels like living, and that has a positive influence on others?

"Your life matters. Be consciously aware of that every day."

- Soul Decisions Coaching

An exercise: your impact

We all impact the world in some way, big or small. How do you impact the world – your closest family and friends, acquaintances at school or university or work, and people you meet in the street?

If you asked your friends, family, and peers about you, what would they say? Try it. You just might learn something new about yourself.

Write down what your loved ones have to say.

"Surround yourself with people who have big ideas and take action on them."

— Soul Decisions Coaching

"What's the point of being alive if you don't at least try to do something remarkable?"

– John Green

"The moment we see ourselves as our own source of inspiration, we begin the journey of mastery of our own thoughts and choices."

- Sharon Pearson

An exercise: being remarkable

What does remarkable mean to you? It could be being a good friend, putting someone else's needs before your own, being a great son or daughter, helping someone, showing compassion for others, making someone smile, or seeing the best in others.

What could you do that is remarkable?

"If you are always trying to fit in or compare yourself to others, you will never realize how amazing you can be."

Soul Decisions Coaching

An exercise: your relationships

Are there some people in your life who drain you of energy? Who you just can't be yourself with? And are there people in your life who you gain energy from? Who let you be who you are and say what you want?

People who drain me:	People who energise me:

It's important to recognize who we've invited into our lives, and how we let our nearest and dearest treat us. Reciprocal relationships are built on total trust and need the same level of investment from both people involved. That's why recognizing the way we treat others is just as important.

Spend more time with the people who energise you, who you just love to spend time with.

Who are your role models, and why? How can you become those things that you admire in that person?

Role Model:	Why:

Things to be aware of when life feels tough

Everything passes with time.

There have been times in your life when things have felt tough, and you've always come through them.

When things don't go the way you expect, maybe that's the universe's way of nudging you towards a new direction.

You have something to learn from every experience.

Let yourself see the gift.

Go and have some fun.

Show yourself compassion and be kind to yourself.

Let go of any negativity from others. It isn't yours to keep.

Let yourself acknowledge the things in your life to be grateful for.

Show kindness and compassion to someone else.

Show love, accept love, radiate love.

"The smallest act of COMPASSION can have the biggest IMPACT."

— Soul Decisions Coaching

Compassion is an incredibly positive emotion that reflects your kindness, thoughtfulness, and understanding of suffering.

Reflect on how you feel when you're kind to yourself. How do you show compassion to yourself?

When we give to other people, we feed our souls. We create more meaning in our lives. Reflect on how you feel when you help someone else. How do you show compassion to the people around you?

"When we believe change is possible, change happens."

Aditi Ishaya

You're not alone.
"No matter how happy someone may seem, they have moments when they question if they can go on.
No matter how confident someone may look, there are times when they feel unsure and insecure.
And no matter how strong someone may appear, they have days when they feel like they're falling apart.
Never think for a moment you're alone with your struggles. You're not a mess. You're human."

Lori Deschene

Conclusion

As I've written this book, I've thought about my amazing children and their wonderful friends. My heart has been filled with love and hope for their success in life. Young souls searching for answers, learning how to exist in this world.

As you've worked through these pages, I hope you've discovered some compelling truths about yourself. I hope you've found a passion for your life that lets you live it to the fullest. I hope it's helped you discover that you're perfect just as you are, with all your own personal quirks and differences that make you unique.

We've covered where to start your discoveries into your inner world, with the desire to make changes in your life. We took a close look at how you live your life now, either above the line or below the line, and how to use that way of thinking to keep yourself in check. We've asked some tough questions to help you dig deep for the answers that you didn't even know were possible. We've uncovered tools that will help you cope when life seems rocky – and if you use them, you will see your life filled with freedom. We've thought in-depth about what you value and believe to be true about your world. About how your relationships are impacted by your values and beliefs and the fact that your thoughts aren't who you are. We dove deep into the inner workings of the ego, to help you to understand how it works both resourcefully and unresourcefully, and how that impacts your quality of life. And along the journey, we've discovered that facing fears, gaining confidence, making decisions, and taking action are all the keys to making change happen.

So now, it's time. Time to stand tall, hold your head high, put your shoulders back, and believe fully in yourself.

You're an amazing human being with your own unique gifts.

Go and be unstoppable.

From my heart and soul to yours with love,
Deb

About Soul Decisions Coaching

Meet Debbie and Becky.
Two sisters, creating connections from opposite corners of the world.

After a challenging childhood in northern England, Debbie and Becky set off on two separate journeys across two different continents. Until, in early 2019, their paths were drawn back together – and they reconnected to form Soul Decisions Coaching. A joint venture based on connection, understanding, excitement, and creativity.

Born from a shared love of Bowen Therapy, Soul Decisions has since grown to include life coaching, meditation, and personal health. Creating the unique opportunity to bring complementary therapies together, and giving clients in Austin, Texas, and Whakatane, New Zealand, the best of both Debbie and Becky's worlds.

With Debbie's big-picture thinking and Becky's grounded mindfulness, Soul Decisions is a meeting of skill-sets and spirits. Fulfilling its purpose of helping their clients live beautiful lives to the very fullest, every single day.

To book an appointment, purchase Soul Decision Coaching's Value Cards and Inspiration Cards, or learn more about Debbie and Becky, visit:

souldecisionscoaching.com

Made in the USA
Monee, IL
08 August 2020